A book
is a present you can open
again and again.

THIS BOOK BELONGS TO

_____

FROM

_____

Anytime Rhymes

RIDDLES & RHYMES

Illustrated by Dick Martin

World Book, Inc.
a Scott Fetzer company
Chicago London Sydney Toronto

Copyright © 1992
World Book, Inc.
525 West Monroe Street
Chicago, Illinois 60661

Printed in the United States of America
ISBN 0-7166-1617-3
Library of Congress Catalog Card No. 91-65752

D/IC

Cover design by Rosa Cabrera
Book design by Valerie Nelson-Metlay

Who's There?

Knock, knock.
  Who's there?
Mister.
  Mister who?
Mister plane and had to take a later flight.

Knock, knock.
   Who's there?
Sherwood.
   Sherwood who?
Sherwood like to get to know you.

Knock, knock.
   Who's there?
Phil.
   Phil who?
Phil like taking a walk?

Knock, knock.
  Who's there?
Howard.
  Howard who?
Howard you like to go swimming?

Knock, knock.
  Who's there?
Wanda.
  Wanda who?
Wanda go to the movies?

Knock, knock.
  Who's there?
Ken.
  Ken who?
Ken you loan me a dollar?

Knock, knock.
  Who's there?
Arthur.
  Arthur who?
Arthur any cookies left?

Knock, knock.
  Who's there?
Banana.
  Banana who?
Knock, knock.
  Who's there?
Banana.
  Banana who?
Knock, knock.
  Who's there?
Banana.
  Banana who?
Knock, knock.
  Who's there?
Orange.
  Orange who?
Orange you glad
    I didn't say banana?

Knock, knock.
  Who's there?
Wooden shoe.
  Wooden shoe who?
Wooden shoe like to have some ice cream?

Knock, knock.
   Who's there?
Shirley.
   Shirley who?
Shirley you know me.

Knock, knock.
   Who's there?
Luke.
   Luke who?
Luke out, there's a monster behind you!

Knock, knock.
  Who's there?
Stu.
  Stu who?
Stu early to go to bed.

Knock, knock.
  Who's there?
Wilma.
  Wilma who?
Wilma dreams come true?

The Riddler

What do you get when you cross
a laughing hyena with a parrot?

an animal that laughs at its own jokes

What do you get when you cross
a kangaroo with an iguana?

leaping lizards

What do you need
to fix a broken
chimpanzee?

a monkey wrench

What do you get when you cross
a sheep with a porcupine?

an animal that knits its own sweaters

What happened when the toucan
put its beak in the electric socket?

It got an electric bill.

How can you tell
when a skunk is angry?

It raises a stink.

Why do leopards have
a hard time hiding?

They are always spotted.

Where do sheep get a haircut?

at the baa baa shop

Why can't you tell
secrets on a farm?

The corn has ears.

Why did the hen
sit on the ax?

to hatchet

Do rabbits comb their hair?

No. They use hare brushes.

When do ducks wake up?

at the quack of dawn

What did the old flower
say to the young flower?

Hello, bud.

What do you call pigs
who write each other letters?

pen pals

Why did the piglet eat so much?

to make a hog of itself

What kind of screen lets
things into your house
instead of keeping them out?

a TV screen

What kind of rooms have
no windows, walls, ceilings,
floors, or doors?

mushrooms

What has a neck
but no head?

a bottle

What kind of shoes can you make out of banana peels?

slippers

Why are the strawberries upset?

because they're in a jam

What has four legs, a back, two arms, but no head or body?

a chair

What happens to a cat when it eats lemons?

It becomes a sour puss.

What do you call a dog that is running a fever?

a hot dog

What is the best fish to have with peanut butter?

jellyfish

What has many holes but can hold water?

a sponge

How do you know
that the sun is
smart?

because it
is very bright

Where do you find oceans without water,
forests without trees, highways without cars,
and cities without people?

on a map

How many times can you
subtract 9 from 99?

Only once. After that it is 90.

How do you get a giant
to understand what
you are saying?

Use big words.

What is the difference between
a teacher and a train?

A teacher says, "Spit out your gum,"
and a train says, "Choo, choo."

What kind of coat has
no buttons or sleeves?

a coat of paint

When does an empty pocket
have something in it?

when it has a hole

What would it be like
to have eight arms?

very handy

Why are spiders good baseball players?

They catch flies.

What has eighteen legs and catches flies?

a baseball team

Who can see an iceberg
that's 20 miles away?

someone with good ice sight

When is snow like a tree?

when it leaves in spring

What kind of ball is fun to play with
even though it doesn't bounce?

a snowball

Which is faster,
hot or cold?

Hot. Anyone can
catch cold.

Riddles in Rhyme

I disguise myself to confuse you,
But once you know me,
I can never fool you.

Find the answers to
Riddles in Rhyme
on last page.

First you see me in the grass,
Dressed in yellow I play.
Next time you see me,
I'm dainty white,
Then I fly away.

I have a mouth,
But speak not a word.
I have no legs,
Yet I can run swiftly.

Never seen,
Only heard,
I only speak when spoken to.

Dart and dash,
Slip and slide.
Where I live,
I also hide.

From house to house I go,
Sometimes narrow, sometimes wide.
And whether there's rain or snow,
I always stay outside.

Lighter than a feather
Yet harder to hold.
You only see me when it is c

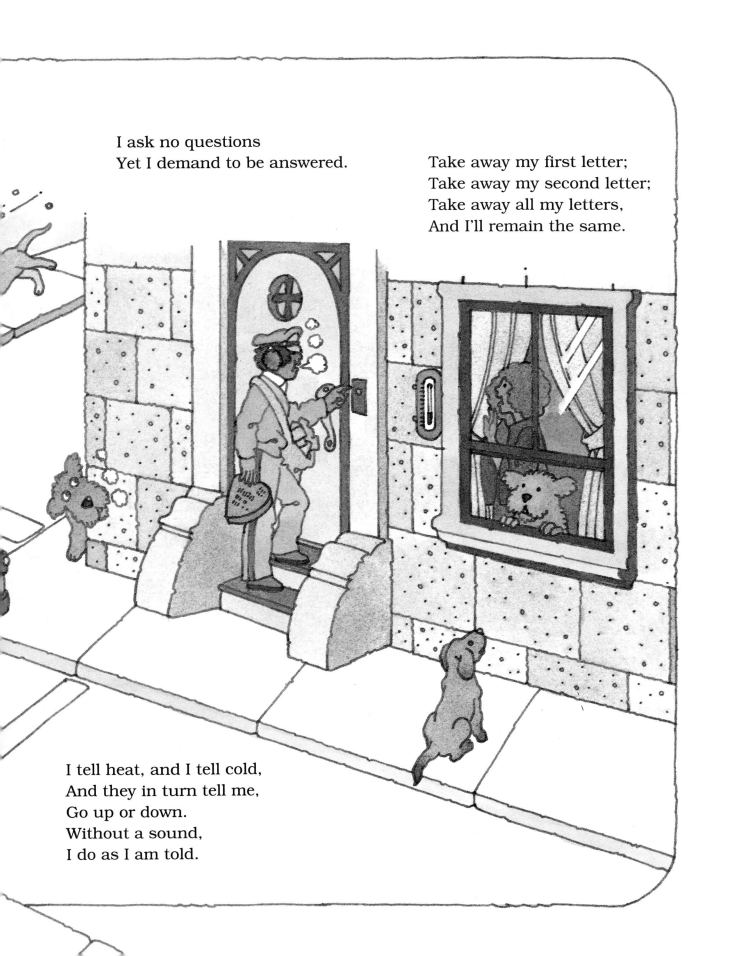

I ask no questions
Yet I demand to be answered.

Take away my first letter;
Take away my second letter;
Take away all my letters,
And I'll remain the same.

I tell heat, and I tell cold,
And they in turn tell me,
Go up or down.
Without a sound,
I do as I am told.

You saw me where I never was,
And where I could not be;
And yet within that very place,
My face you often see.

Look in my face,
I am somebody.
Look in my back,
I am nobody.

Thirty-two horses on a red hill.
Now they stampede,
And now stand still.

Though I have many teeth,
I cannot eat.

We are a pair,
We can dart here and there,
Though we always stay in one place.
We can smile, shed tears,
Show our pleasure or fears,
And are found on everyone's face.

I come with the train.
I go with the train.
I am of no use to the train,
Yet the train cannot go without me.

I appear once in a minute,
Once in a blue moon,
Yet never in one hundred years.

'Tis true I have both face and hands,
And move before your eyes;
When I go, my body stands,
And when I stand, I lie.

A houseful,
A roomful,
Can't catch a spoonful.

One man can carry me.
Yet not even a hundred men
Can make me stand on end.

Answers to Riddles in Rhyme

I disguise myself to confuse you,
But once you know me,
I can never fool you. (a riddle)

First you see me in the grass,
Dressed in yellow I play.
Next time you see me, I'm dainty white,
Then I fly away. (a dandelion)

I have a mouth,
But speak not a word.
I have no legs,
Yet I can run swiftly. (a river)

Never seen,
Only heard,
I only speak when spoken to. (an echo)

Dart and dash,
Slip and slide.
Where I live,
I also hide. (a fish)

From house to house I go,
Sometimes narrow, sometimes wide.
And whether there's rain or snow,
I always stay outside. (a road)

Lighter than a feather
Yet harder to hold.
You only see me when it is cold. (breath)

I ask no questions
Yet I demand to be answered. (doorbell)

I tell heat, and I tell cold,
And they in turn tell me,
Go up or down.
Without a sound,
I do as I am told. (mercury in a thermometer)

Take away my first letter;
Take away my second letter;
Take away all my letters,
And I'll remain the same. (a letter carrier)

You saw me where I never was,
And where I could not be;
And yet within that very place,
My face you often see. (reflection in a mirror)

Look in my face,
I am somebody.
Look in my back,
I am nobody. (a mirror)

Thirty-two horses on a red hill.
Now they stampede,
And now stand still. (teeth)

Though I have many teeth,
I cannot eat. (a comb)

We are a pair,
We can dart here and there,
Though we always stay in one place.
We can smile, shed tears,
Show our pleasure or fears,
And are found on everyone's face. (eyes)

I come with the train.
I go with the train.
I am of no use to the train,
Yet the train cannot go without me. (noise)

I appear once in a minute,
Once in a blue moon,
Yet never in one hundred years. (the letter m)

'Tis true I have both face and hands,
And move before your eyes;
When I go, my body stands,
And when I stand, I lie. (a clock)

A houseful,
A roomful,
Can't catch a spoonful. (smoke)

One man can carry me.
Yet not even a hundred men
Can make me stand on end. (a rope)

To Parents

Children delight in hearing and reading riddles and jokes. The collection featured in *Riddles & Rhymes* will amuse your child and provide a bridge into learning some important concepts. Here are a few easy and natural ways your child can express feelings and understandings about the collection. You know your child and can best judge which ideas he or she will enjoy most.

Note: Some of these activities involve retelling riddles and jokes or making up new ones. Don't be concerned with how accurate or sensible the riddles and jokes are. Simply let your child enjoy experimenting.

Encourage your child to tell favorite riddles and jokes to family members and friends.

Use a mystery box to help your child discover and describe the properties of different objects. Put one object at a time in a shoebox. Have your child tap the box and say, "Knock knock, what's there?" Then have your child shut her or his eyes and open the box. Encourage your child to describe how the object feels and to draw conclusions about what it could be and why.

Play a game of "Name That Riddle" with your child. Take turns randomly reading the answer to a riddle or joke. The listener has to remember the riddle or make up a new one.

Let your child choose a favorite riddle or joke to illustrate. For example, write a riddle on one side of the paper and its answer on the other. Have your child decorate both sides of the paper. Then attach a piece of yarn or string and hang the riddle or joke from a light fixture or a door frame.

Encourage your child to make up "knock, knock" jokes with the names of family members and friends, and to make up other riddles and jokes as well. They might be about things in your home, neighborhood, or school. In a notebook, write down the riddles and jokes that get the biggest laughs so that they will be remembered.